SHAPES

FIRST MATHS

©2017
Book Life
King's Lynn
Norfolk PE30 4LS

ISBN: 978-1-78637-121-8

Written by:
Joanna Brundle

Designed by:
Danielle Jones

A catalogue record for this book
is available from the British Library

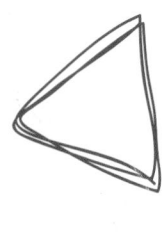

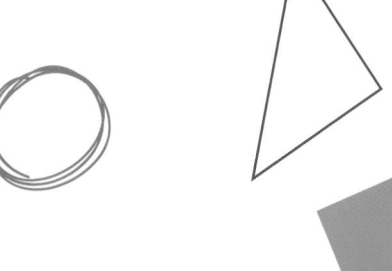
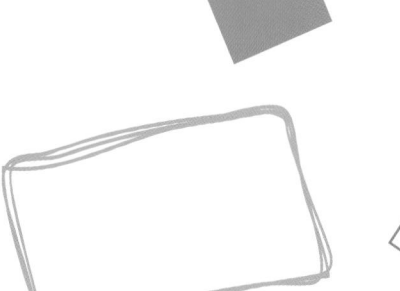
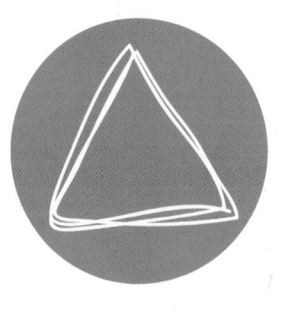

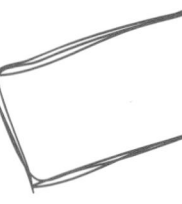

PHOTO CREDITS

**Abbreviations: l-left, r-right, b-bottom,
t-top, c-centre, m-middle.**

Front cover – Gladskikh Tatiana. 3 – Bloomua. 5 – Robert Anthony. 6 – ideldesign. 7 – Dmitry Naumov. 9 – Nicolesa. 10 – izzzy71. 11 – omphoto. 13 – Di Studio. 14 – ChameleonsEye.
15 – SOMMAI. 17 – witittorn onkhaw. 18 – ADfoto. 22 – Peter Vrabel. 23 – MAGRIT HIRSCH.

Images are courtesy of Shutterstock.com. With thanks to Getty Images, Thinkstock Photo and iStockphoto.

CONTENTS

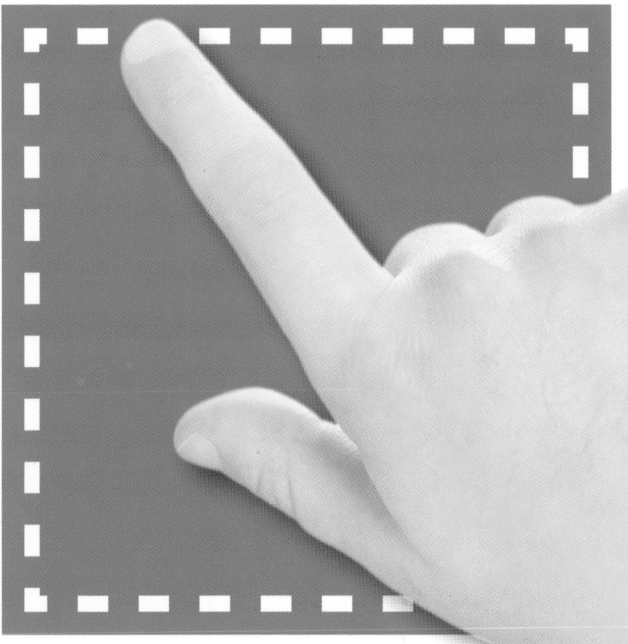

Trace the shapes with your finger as you read.

SQUARES

Side

Corner

A square has four sides and four corners.

A window can be a square.

Tiles can be squares.

RECTANGLES

Count the sides.

Count the corners.

A rectangle has four sides and four corners.

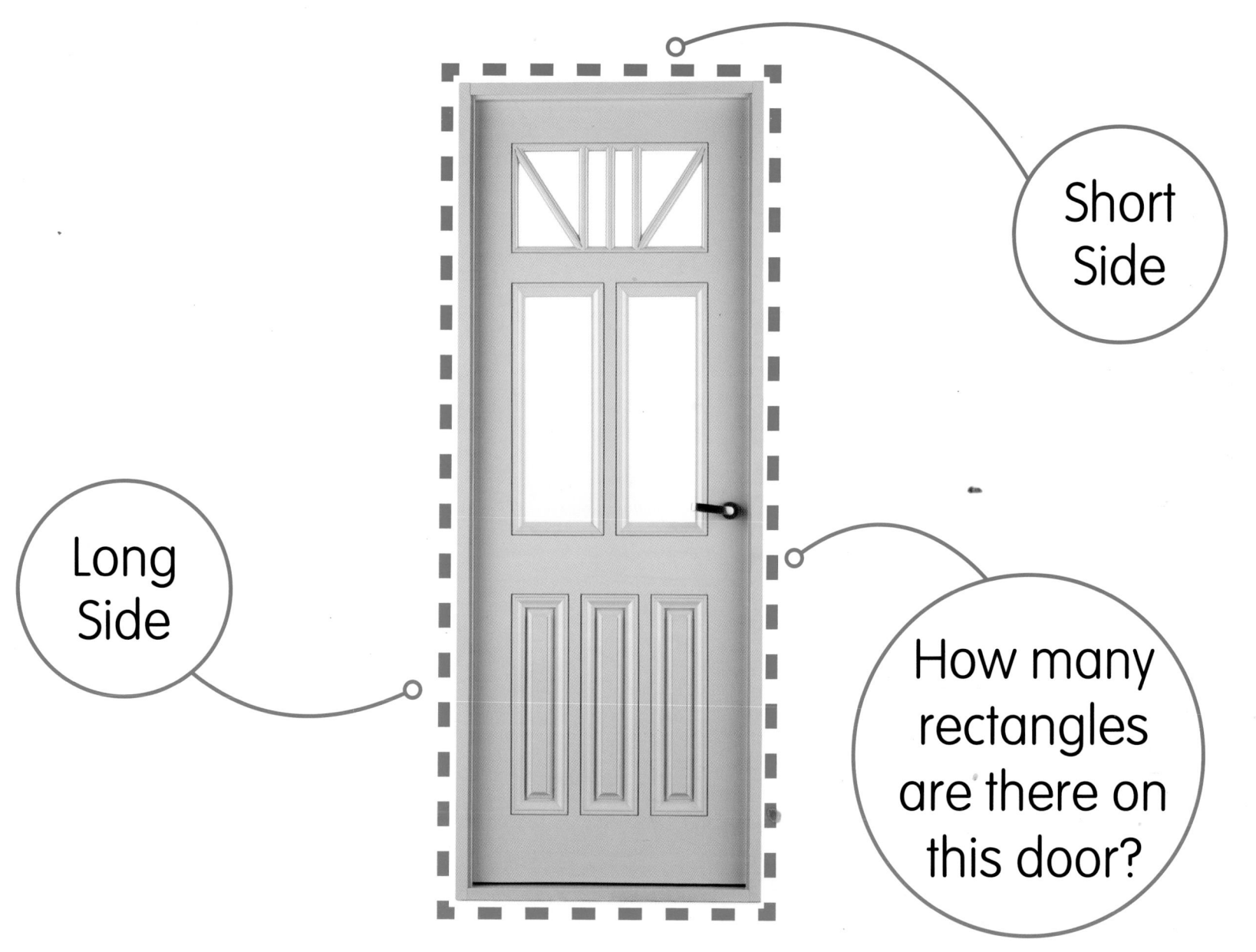

Short Side

Long Side

How many rectangles are there on this door?

A rectangle has two short sides and two long sides.

Happy Birthday!

A birthday card can be a rectangle.

A chocolate bar can be a rectangle.

CIRCLES

Curved Edge

A circle is round. It has a curved edge.

A clock can be a circle.

A circle has no sides and no corners.

You can see circles on a tree stump.

Cucumber slices are circles.

15

TRIANGLES

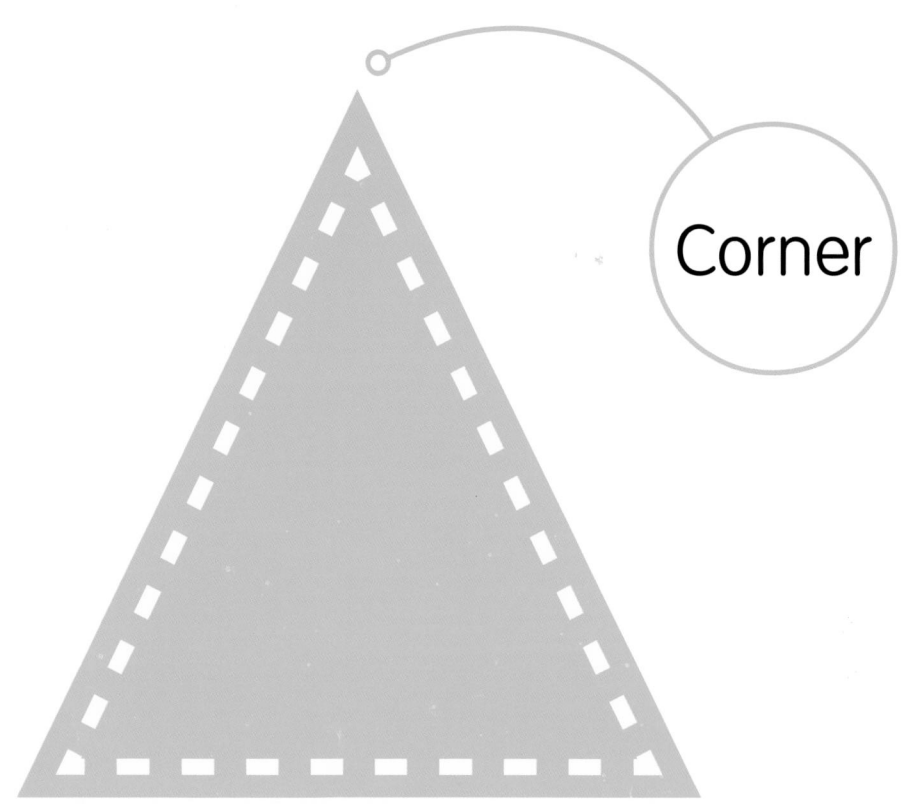

Corner

A triangle has three sides and three corners.

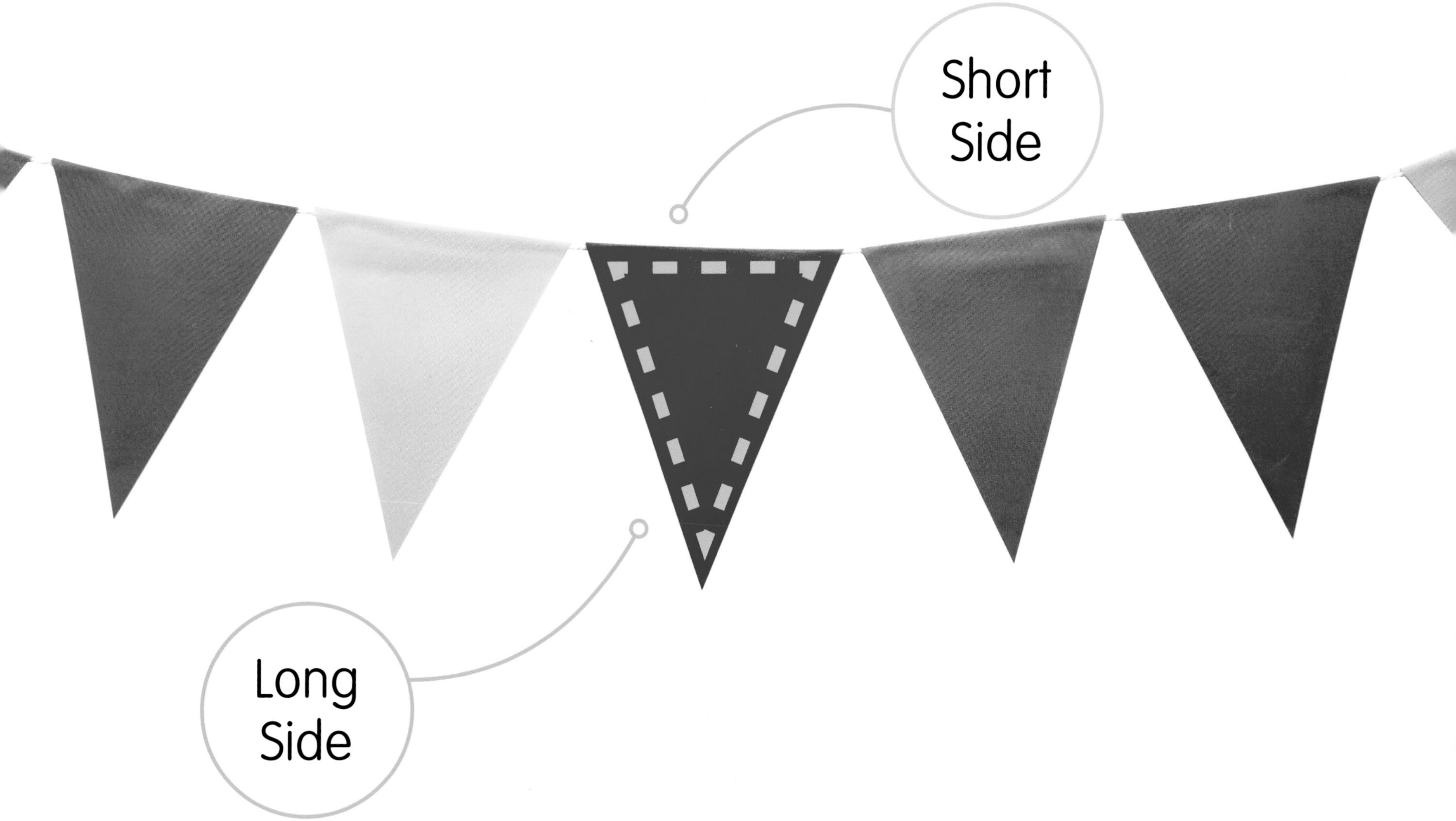

Short
Side

Long
Side

The sides can be the same size or different sizes.

A pizza slice can be a triangle.

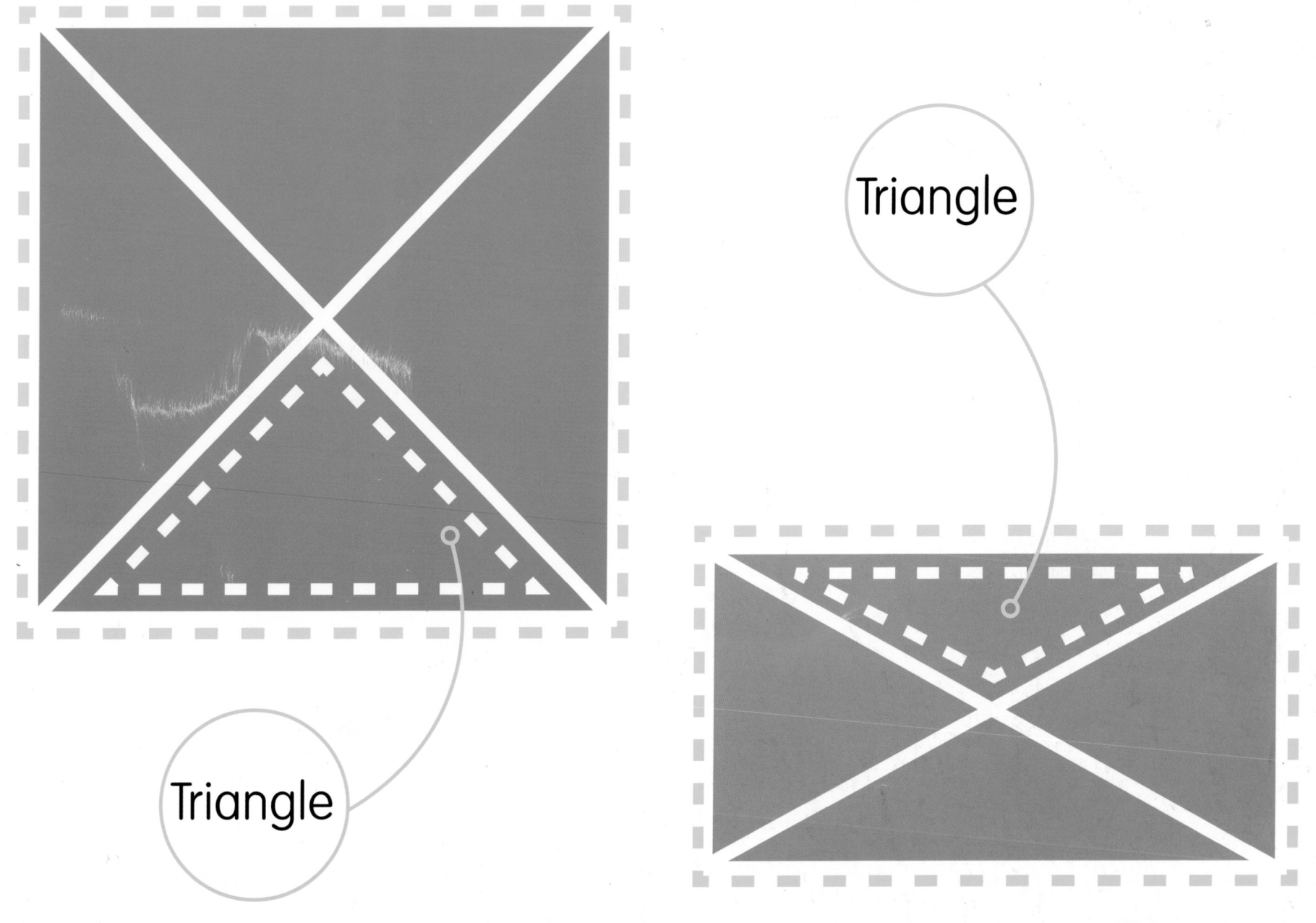

Triangle

Triangle

Four triangles can make a square or a rectangle.

OTHER SHAPES

Oval

Diamond

Do you know what these shapes are?

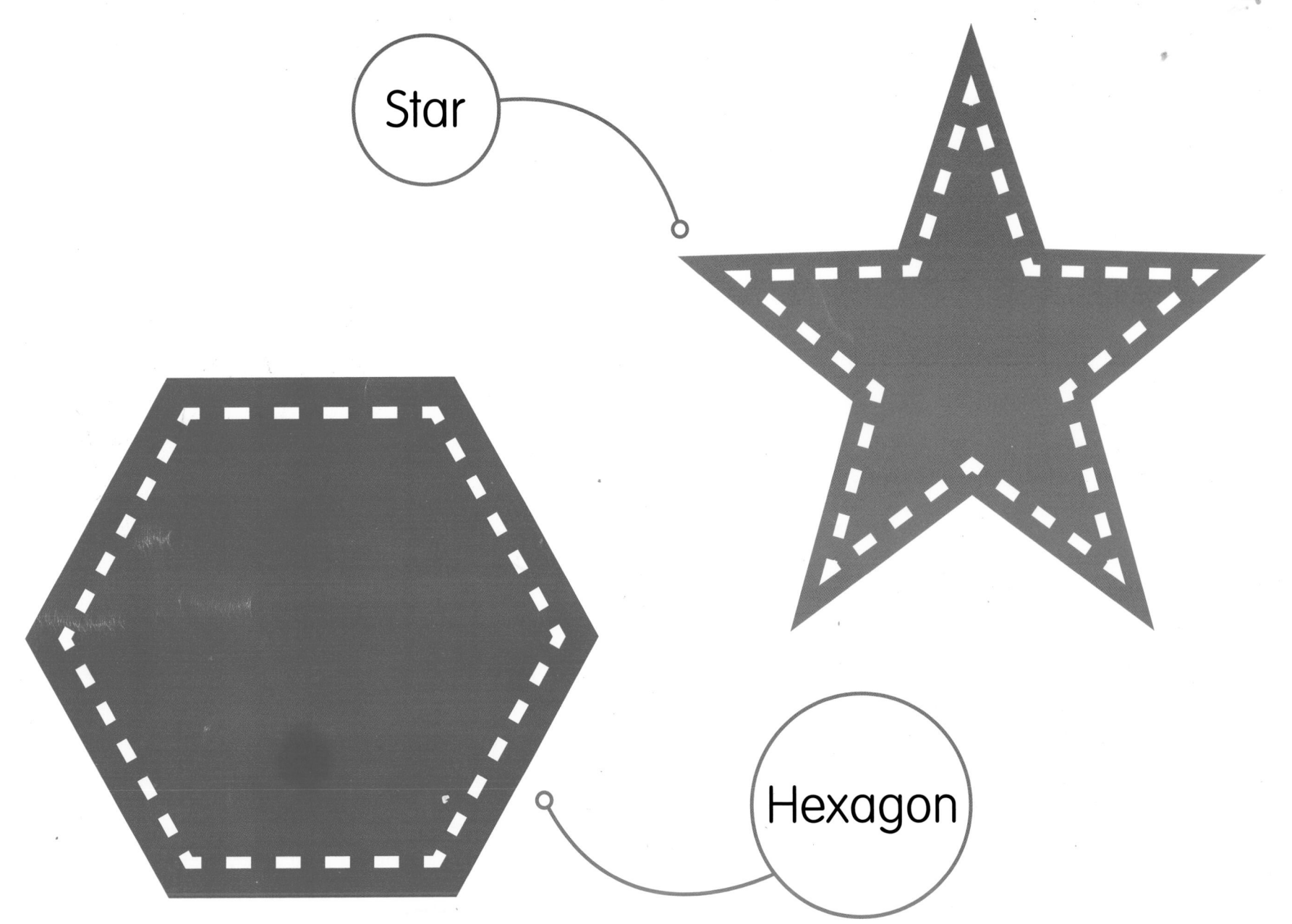

Star

Hexagon

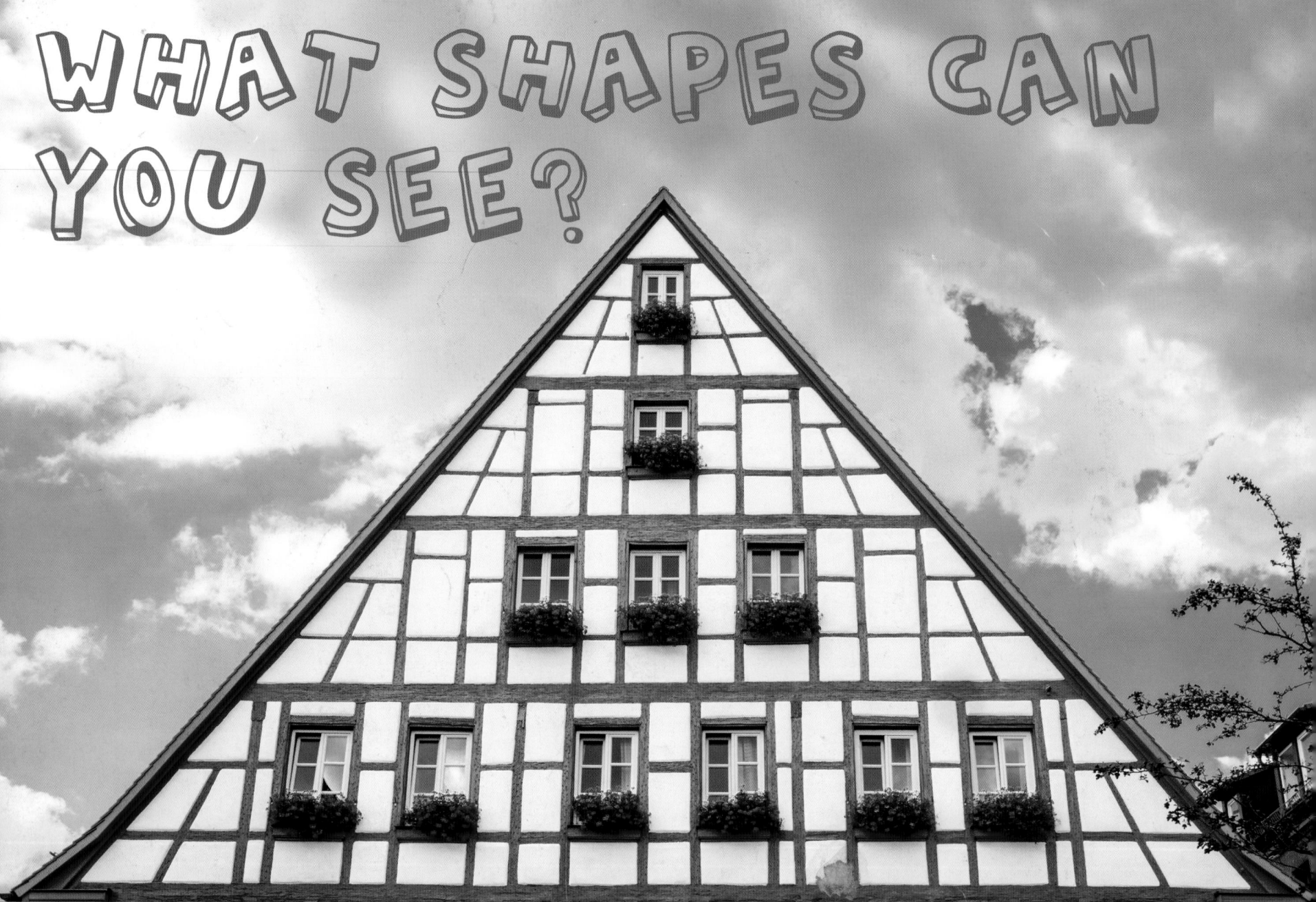

WHAT SHAPES CAN YOU SEE?

What shapes can you see on this house?

Answers on page 24.

What shapes can you see on this quilt?

23

ANSWERS

HOUSE: Triangles, rectangles, squares

QUILT: Rectangles, squares, triangles, diamonds